THIS BOOK BELONGS TO

Manufactured by Amazon.ca
Bolton, ON

43952594R00061